Today's Globalization

A Toolkit for Popular Education in Your Community

Based on workshops created and conducted by Project South Staff

Written and Edited by Project South Staff & Board

Design by Emery Wright & Diamond Lounge Creative, LLC

2nd Edition
Spring 2005

ISBN
1-932085-15-7

Project South: Institute for the Elimination of Poverty & Genocide

9 Gammon Avenue
Atlanta, GA 30315
404 622-0602 phone
404 622-6618 fax
general-info@projectsouth.org

www.projectsouth.org

Acknowledgements

The second edition of Today's Globalization "toolkit" is being published while global forms of oppression are affecting our lives at the grassroots in very real ways. In compiling and editing information to include in this toolkit, we had to make choices. How do you choose which oppression or issue to lift up? Especially when the global elite is consistently dividing our communities and struggles. For example, here in the US South, the Prison Industrial Complex is out-of-control. From the police, to the courts and prison system, the target is Black people, Latinos, people without a lot of money and young people. But how does that compare to the AIDS pandemic in Africa? Both issues are the result of globalization today. Both issues call for genuine concern and effective action.

In developing Today's Globalization toolkit we looked at examples of both top-down global-ization and bottom-up movement building. We compiled history to give context to these examples; we tried to pay close attention to the left out, marginalized people and regions. However, we are based in the US South and Today's Globalization is limited to a US focus. As we publish this toolkit there is 1 significant issue that is both global and relevant to people living in America. The US-led Occupation and War in Iraq. This war has killed and caused suffering for millions of Iraqis. We acknowledge this intolerable injustice and dedicate the second edition of Today's Globalization to the Iraqi people and their struggle. May justice prevail!

Communities in struggle asked "what is globalization?" and "how does this affect us?" This toolkit (and all our publications) is our humble attempt to respond to those questions and lift up the courageous work of those who have come before us. It is critical to acknowledge these many communities. Resiliency and the ability to bounce back from adversity, has been their gift to our current struggles, and we pay honor and respect to all those who have been in struggle from our past to our present.

The process of updating this toolkit involved many people, who worked to compile, re-design and edit a lot of different material. Project South staff, board, membership and friends all contributed in many ways. I would like to thank this Project South crew, past and present, for all their contributions. Specifically: Jerome Scott and Walda Katz-Fishman for their article and other pieces they wrote; Stephanie Guilloud for her help with both con-tent and editing. Lisa Albrecht and Walda Katz-Fishman for their many edits; and Will Cordery, Shella Fon and Christi Ketchum for their feedback and additions.

Other people that deserve a shout-out for design, advice, and feedback include: Tyler Askew, Seth Markle, Dustin Ross, Dana Wright, Kenny Bailey, Najma Nazy'at, Jozan Powell, Ndungi Githuku, Njuguna Mutahi, Tufara Waller Muhammad, Dan Horowitz de Garcia, Up & Out of Poverty Now! Coalition, Georgia Coalition on Hunger, Georgia Human Rights Union, Grassroots Global Justice, COMPA, our other partner organizations and many others!

Peace and Respect,

Emery Wright, Program Director Project South
Spring 2005

Project South: Institute for the Elimination of Poverty & Genocide